Contents

Introduction

'But who are you? I've never seen anyone like you before. My name's John Ridd. What's your name?'

'Lorna Doone.'

Doone! To me, the name was terrible! She was one of the Doones who had killed my father. But her voice touched my heart and I could not hate her. Her beautiful hair fell down on to her shoulders. There were lights and shadows in her eyes, like sunlight in a deep forest.

In 1673, in a high, wild valley, young John Ridd, a farmer's son, meets a gentle little girl called Lorna Doone. The Doones are a family of robbers and murderers. One of them, Carver Doone, is the killer of John Ridd's father. The boy leaves the valley, but he cannot forget Lorna. Seven years later, he returns to the valley as a young man and meets her again. She is now a beautiful young woman, and the two start meeting secretly. But Lorna is not allowed to leave the Doone valley. Carver Doone wants her to be his wife, and if she refuses, he will force her to marry him.

John is ordered to go to London. A rebellion against the king is planned, and the government want information from John about it. They also want him to help destroy the Doones. But can John destroy the Doones and save Lorna?

The writer of this book, Richard Doddridge Blackmore, was born in 1825. He went to school in Tiverton, where we meet John Ridd in the first chapter of this book.

Blackmore went to Oxford University and then studied law. He worked as a lawyer in London for a few years. But then illness forced him to live in the country and he started growing and selling flowers, fruit and vegetables. At the same time, he wrote poems, but not very successfully. His first book, *Clara Vaughan*, was much more successful when it appeared in 1864.

Lorna Doone came out in 1869. It was very long, and at first it was not a great success. To Blackmore's surprise, though, it slowly became more popular. Then in 1871, the book was made shorter and it was sold more cheaply. In that same year, Princess Louise, a daughter of Queen Victoria, married a man who was not from the royal family. People became very excited about the wedding. A journalist compared the royal marriage to the story in *Lorna Doone*. After that, everyone wanted to read the book. Today, it is still a well-loved story.

Blackmore wrote several other books, but we remember him for *Lorna Doone*. Lorna became a very popular name for girls. The writer had no children, and died in 1900.

In 1673, when the story of *Lorna Doone* begins, Charles II was king of England. He and his wife had no children, and when he died in 1685 his brother, James II, became king. But many people did not like James, because he did not share the same religion as his brother. These people wanted another man, the Duke of Monmouth, to be king. The Duke was Charles II's son, but Charles had not married the Duke's mother.

When James II became king, the Duke of Monmouth was living in France. Four months after Charles's death, the Duke arrived in Dorset, in south-west England. Many people from south-west England fought for the duke. But they were not soldiers, and James II's army beat them very easily. This battle is described in *Lorna Doone*. The Duke of Monmouth was taken to court and killed. Many of his supporters were punished by Judge Jeffreys, who was known as 'the hanging judge', and who also appears in this book.

In this story, the Doone valley is in Exmoor, in the west of England. Exmoor lies across the counties of Somerset and Devon. Most of it is high land, sometimes more than 1,600 feet. It is about twenty-one miles from east to west, and about twelve miles from north to south. In the higher parts there are no trees, only low bushes, rock and marshes. There are some very beautiful valleys in Exmoor, and in one of them lies the village of Oare, which really exists.

Chapter 1   John Ridd

My name is John Ridd. My home is in Oare, a village in the county of Somerset, in the south-west of England. My father was a farmer, and we owned a large farm, which had been in our family for hundreds of years. We were not rich, but we lived very comfortably.

I was the only boy in our family, and my father wanted me to go to a good school. He sent me to Tiverton School in Devon, the county next to Somerset. It was the largest school in the west of England.

My story begins on 29th November 1673, my twelfth birthday. My friends and I came out of school at five o'clock and saw a long line of horses coming down the road. The horses were carrying gold, and the gold was guarded by soldiers because a famous highwayman was in the area. I was very interested when I heard this; the highwayman, whose name was Tom Faggus, was my cousin.

We all ran to the gate to see the soldiers pass. Just then a man on horseback came round the corner, leading another horse behind him.

'Have any of you seen John Ridd?' he asked.

The man was John Fry, a servant at our home. I went forward and spoke to him.

'John!' I cried. 'Why have you come now? School doesn't finish for another two weeks.'

John Fry turned his eyes away from me.

'I know that,' he said. 'But your mother wants you at home—' He stopped suddenly, and this frightened me.

'And Father – how's Father?' I asked. 'He always comes to take me home from school.'

'Oh – he was too busy to come,' said John Fry.

He was looking at the ground as he said this, and I knew that something was wrong. I was very worried, but I went with him. We left Tiverton early the next morning.

◆

It is a long and difficult journey from Tiverton to Oare because the road crosses Exmoor, a large area of high, wild land. There are marshes there, and it is often difficult to find the road. We crossed two rivers, and it was midday when we reached the town of Dulverton. We talked as we travelled, and I knew that John Fry was lying to me about my father. He did not want to tell me why I had to return home from school.

At Dulverton we had lunch in a pub, and afterwards I went outside to wash. A young woman came out of the house and watched me.

'Come here, little boy,' she said in a foreign accent. 'Your eyes are so blue! Your skin is like snow!'

I felt very embarrassed. 'I'm sorry, madam, I must go,' I said.

'Then go, my dear. My name is Benita, and I'm the servant of a great lady. Can you tell me how far it is to the village of Watchet?'

'Oh, it's a long way,' I said, 'and the road is as bad as the road to Oare.'

'Oare – is that where you live? I'll remember that. Perhaps one day I'll come and look for you there. Now please fill this glass with water for my lady.'

I filled the glass and she went back inside.

John Fry and I started our journey again about an hour later. After we had travelled some distance, we passed a big carriage with six horses going up a hill. In the carriage I saw the servant that I had met outside the pub. There was also a woman with a lovely, kind face and a pretty little girl with wonderful dark hair. I took off my hat to them, and the woman waved her hand to me.

We did not see them again because we turned off on to a side road and rode over the moor. The road got worse and worse, and soon there was none at all. Thick mist came down and we could not see beyond our horses' heads. When the mist cleared for a moment, I saw a terrible sight. A man was hanging from the tree in front of me. My heart felt cold with fear.

'Who's that hanging from the tree?' I asked. 'Have they hanged one of the Doones, John?'

'Hanged one of the Doones!' said John. 'Don't be so stupid! Even the king wouldn't dare to hang one of the Doones. No, that's only a thief called Red Jem.'

We continued our journey. I wanted to know more about the thief.

'Who was Red Jem?' I asked.

'Be quiet!' he said. 'We're near the Doones' path now. It's the highest place on the moor. If they're out tonight, we must go quietly.'

The Doones! Thieves, murderers and outlaws, the Doones of Bagworthy were hated and feared by everyone in Devon and Somerset. My legs began to shake.

'But, John,' I whispered, 'they won't see us in this thick mist, will they?'

'They can see through any mist,' said John. 'God never made a mist thick enough to stop their eyes. Now go quietly, boy, if you want to live to see your mother.'

We rode down the side of a deep valley and up the other side. Then I heard a frightening noise. It was the sound of horses' feet and the breathing of tired men.

'Get off your horse,' said John in a low voice. 'Let the horse go free.'

We lay down on the ground behind a small tree on the hillside. I saw the first horseman pass on the path below me.

Suddenly the mist cleared and a red light appeared.

'That's the fire on Dunkery Hill,' said John in my ear. 'They light it to show the Doones the way home.'

I lay only a few feet above the heads of the riders. They were big, heavy men, more than thirty of them, with long boots and leather jackets, and they carried guns. Their horses were carrying the things that they had stolen. I could see cups made of silver and gold, bags, boxes and dead sheep.

One man had a child lying across his horse. The child wore a beautiful dress, and it shone in the firelight. I felt very sad when I saw this, and I wondered what would happen to the child.

When the men had gone, we continued our journey, silent and shocked. At last we reached the house, but my father did not come to meet me. At first, I thought that perhaps he had guests. But then, I don't know how, I understood. I went away to hide, to be alone. I did not want to hear it.

After some time, I heard the sound of weeping. Then my mother and sister appeared, holding each other. I could not look at them, and turned away.

My father was dead. He had been killed by the Doones.

He was riding home from market with five other farmers. Suddenly a Doone had appeared in front of them, and demanded all their money. The five farmers began to look for their money, but my father had attacked the robber with his stick.

Then twelve more of the Doones appeared and attacked my father. He struck down three of them, but one man, Carver Doone, had a gun and shot my father. The next morning my father was found dead on the moor with his stick under him.

My father was dead, and now I had to be the man of the family. My mother was very shocked by my father's death, but I knew that she would be able to manage the farm. But legally, the farm was mine, and my mother and my two sisters, Annie and little Lizzie, were my responsibility.

♦

I must explain who the Doones were, and how they came to Bagworthy.

In the year 1640, two men owned a large amount of land in the north of England. One was a very clever man called Sir Ensor Doone; the other was his cousin, Lord Lorne. The two men owned the land together, and each man received half of the money that came from it. But Lord Lorne decided that he did not want the money; he wanted half the land. Sir Ensor refused to give it to him. They went to the courts of law in London and asked a judge to make a decision. The judge decided that the land did not belong to either of them.

Although Lord Lorne lost a lot of money, he was still rich. But the judge's decision made Sir Ensor a poor man, and he became very angry. I do not know exactly what he did, but it was something very violent and wrong. Some people say that he killed someone.

The courts made Sir Ensor an outlaw. So he searched for the wildest part of England that he could find. In Bagworthy, on Exmoor, he found a valley with high walls of rock all around it, and he decided to live there.

When he arrived, Sir Ensor had only twelve people with him, including his wife and sons. But, as time passed, others joined him. At first, the Doones lived peacefully and did not harm anyone. The farmers and country people knew Sir Ensor's story and were sorry for him. But then the Doones began to steal from the farmers and from travellers on the roads, and if a man fought them, he was killed. All the Doones were taught to shoot when they were children. People started to hate and fear the Doones, but they did not dare to attack them.

♦

I was only a boy when my father died, but I took my father's gun and taught myself to shoot with it. I had a secret plan. One day, when I was older, I intended to kill the man who had killed my father. I intended to kill Carver Doone.

Chapter 2   Lorna Doone

There are two rivers near our farm – the Bagworthy river and the Lynn. About two miles below our farm, the Bagworthy joins the Lynn, making one wide stream. This stream runs past high hills and through dark woods. It makes little lakes where there are fish. Sometimes, in the summer, I went alone to catch fish, and sometimes I went with my sister Annie.

At fourteen years old, I was very big for my age. Other boys laughed at my size, but they did not want to make me angry because I was strong too. When I fought another boy, I always beat him.

One cold spring morning, I went out to catch fish for my mother. I hung my shoes around my neck and started to walk up a stream that ran near the farm. I went about two miles up the stream, but did not catch any fish. Then I came to a place where the stream was wider and colder. I had caught no fish and I wanted to go home. I took out bread and meat from my bag and began to eat it. As I ate, I began to feel stronger, and I decided to go up the Bagworthy stream as far as the Doone valley. It was a small decision, but it changed my life completely.

The water in this stream was very cold. There were dark places under the trees which filled my heart with fear. But I found a lot of fish. I did not think about the time, but went farther and farther up the stream. I shouted happily when I caught a fish, and my voice came back to me from the hills. There was no other sound in the cold, quiet air.

*One cold spring morning, I went out to catch fish
for my mother.*

The country around me got hillier, with high rocks on either side of the stream. I came to an opening in the trees and saw in front of me a pool of deep, black water. It was a whirlpool and the water went round and round, very fast. I looked up at the high rock on the other side and saw a clear stream of water falling down over the rock. It was a beautiful sight. I wanted to climb to the top and find out why the water came down like that.

I put the fish in a bag round my neck and stood on a rock by the pool. But the rock was green and wet, and I fell into the water. I swam hard but I was carried out, away from the rock, and I could not get back to it.

I was very frightened because by now I was near the bottom of the waterfall. I reached out to some rocks and, with great difficulty, I managed to pull myself out. Then I looked around. The wall of rock around the waterfall went straight up. I could not walk round to the place where I had entered the water. But it was too dangerous to go back into the water.

Looking closely at the waterfall, I saw that there was space between the water and the rock behind it. I could climb up the rock to the top of the waterfall. It was dangerous, and if I fell I would die, but I had no choice. I began to climb, very slowly. The water fell a few inches from my body, the sharp rocks cut my feet and my legs shook with fear, but I climbed up and up. Suddenly I felt fresh air and climbed faster until I fell onto grass.

When I opened my eyes, I saw a little girl by my side.

'Oh, I'm so glad,' she whispered softly, as I looked at her. 'You will be all right now, won't you?'

I had never heard a sweeter voice. I had never seen anything as beautiful as her dark eyes and thick dark hair. I thought of her then as a beautiful spring flower. Now, when I see a spring flower, I still think of her. Perhaps she liked my face too. She told me afterwards that she did.

I sat up.

When I opened my eyes, I saw a little girl. . .

'What's your name?' she asked. 'How did you come here? And what have you got in your bag?'

'They're fish for my mother, but I'll give you some, if you want.'

'Oh, you've hurt your feet!' she cried. 'And you have no shoes. Is your mother very poor, boy?'

'No,' I answered crossly. 'We could buy this whole field if we wanted to. My shoes are in this other bag. But who are you? I've never seen anyone like you before. My name's John Ridd. What's your name?'

'Lorna Doone.'

Doone! To me, the name was terrible! She was one of the Doones who had killed my father. But her voice touched my heart and I could not hate her. Her beautiful hair fell down on to her shoulders. There were lights and shadows in her eyes, like sunlight in a deep forest.

I stood up and touched her hand and tried to make her look at me. But she turned away and started to cry; she was so ashamed of her name.

'Don't cry,' I said, 'I'm sure you've never hurt anyone. I'll give you all my fish, Lorna, and catch some more for Mother. But don't cry.'

'Why did you come here?' she asked. 'The Doones would kill us both if they found you here with me.'

'They wouldn't dare to kill you.'

'They would. They'd kill us both and throw our bodies into the water,' she said.

'Why?' I asked.

'Because you've found the secret way into the Doone valley. They'd think I showed you the way. Now please go, please go! I like you very much, and I'll call you "John", if you like. When your feet are better, you can come and see me.'

'I like you, Lorna. I like you nearly as much as my sister Annie, and more than my sister Lizzie. I've never seen anyone like you. I'll come again tomorrow, and bring you apples and a little dog.'

'Oh, they won't let me have a dog,' she said. 'There isn't a dog in the whole valley.'

'Put your hand in mine,' I said. 'You're such a little thing.'

Suddenly, someone shouted down in the valley. My heart started beating fast, and the little girl's face turned white with fear.

'Oh,' she cried, 'save me!'

'Come with me. We can climb down the back of the waterfall!'

'No, no!' she said. 'They'll see us crossing the grass. Can you see that hole there, near those bushes? There's a way out of the valley through that hole.'

I saw ten or twelve men coming down the valley. I quickly jumped down to the edge of the stream and pulled Lorna after me.

'Queen! Queen!' the men shouted. 'Where have you gone?'

'They always call me "Queen",' the little girl whispered. 'I'll be queen of the valley when I am older.'

'Listen,' I said quickly. 'I'll hide in the water. You lie on the grass over there and pretend to be asleep.'

Lorna ran about a hundred feet to a large rock and lay down, while I lay down in the water. Only my nose showed among the tall grasses. Soon, one of the big men came round the corner. He stopped and looked at Lorna for a moment, then picked her up in his arms.

'Here's our queen,' he shouted. 'Here's our captain's daughter.'

He put her on his shoulder, and the men went back down the valley. I waited, then went to the hole in the rock that Lorna had pointed to. It was as black as night, but I climbed inside it. It was smooth and narrow and very steep. I went very fast – almost fell – down a long, dark passage which brought me out at the edge of the whirlpool. I climbed out and looked back up the hole. I

11

could see no light at the end of it. The passage was very smooth and steep, and I knew that I could not climb up into the valley this way.

Chapter 3   Tom and Winnie

After my visit to the Doone valley, I often thought of Lorna and dreamed about her, but I was too afraid to return to the valley. I grew taller and stronger, and learned to use a gun well. Time goes quickly when you have a lot of work, and there was always a lot of work on the farm.

A year passed. In November there was heavy rain, and the river became very wide and deep. One day, the ducks began to make a great noise. My sister, Annie, and I ran down to the river. A long, thick branch lay across the stream, and one of the ducks was caught in it. The water was rushing over it, and we knew that the duck would drown in a few minutes. Annie started to cry, and I prepared to jump into the water.

Suddenly a man on horseback came round the corner. He understood the situation immediately. 'Get back, boy!' he cried. 'The water will carry you away! *I'll* go in.'

Then he whispered something in the horse's ear, and the beautiful animal went into the rushing water. She swam to the branch and the man pulled the duck free. The water carried them a short distance, and then the horse and rider climbed out.

The man gave me the duck and I looked gratefully at him. He was about twenty-four years old, and had a short, strong body and friendly blue eyes.

'What are you looking at?' he asked. 'I'm your mother's cousin, boy. Tom Faggus is my name, and this is my horse, Winnie.'

Why had I not realized that before? He was Tom Faggus, my highwayman cousin. He and his horse were famous. He had been

Suddenly a man on horseback came round the corner.

a farmer in North Devon, and a popular man, but a rich man had cheated him and taken his land. Now Tom was a highwayman. He stopped travellers on the road and took money from them. But if he liked someone, he gave them their money back, and he often gave money to the poor and the sick.

Annie and I stood looking at Winnie, Tom's horse. We had heard many stories about her. People said that only Tom could ride her.

Tom saw our stares. 'Do you think you could ride my horse?' he asked me.

'I'll try,' I said.

'Well,' he said, 'if you fall, the ground's soft here.'

I got up on the horse's back. Tom gave a short, clear cry and the horse went faster and faster. Then he gave another cry, and the horse tried to throw me off her back, but I held on. The horse jumped higher and tried harder, but I still held on. Then Tom gave another cry and the horse turned back towards him. Then, as she came to the gate of our farm, she threw me off her back.

'Well done!' smiled Tom. 'I didn't think you could stay on so long. I'll buy a new gun for you.'

He rode away, and some weeks later a man came with a new gun for me. I learned to shoot very well with it.

◆

Six years passed. I grew up and became a young man, and I worked very hard on the farm. I grew in size until I was the largest man in Somerset and Devon. Even the Doones were not as big, except, people said, for Carver Doone. I wrestled with other men, and I had to be very careful not to break their bones. I am only telling you these things because my mother and Annie were very proud of me.

Chapter 4   Uncle Reuben

My mother's uncle, Reuben Huckaback, owned the largest shop in Dulverton, and sold clothes around the whole area. We were his only relatives, and my mother thought that we should be friendly to him.

Uncle Reuben came to us every year for New Year's Day. He travelled early in the morning, because that was the best time to escape the Doones. (The Doones were lazy and did not get up until midday. They usually went out in the late afternoon or at night.) But this New Year's Day, the Doones rode out early. They were not interested in stealing, only in having some fun.

We waited for Uncle Reuben until one o'clock, but he did not appear. There was a very thick mist, and we could not see ten feet in front of us. My mother became very anxious.

'Oh John, John,' she said, 'I think those people have got your uncle.'

Mother could never say the word 'Doones'. She always called them 'those people'.

I answered, 'I feel sorry for them. If they catch Uncle Reuben, he'll just build another shop beside the river in their valley. He'll soon take all their money away from them.'

My mother laughed. We decided that we could not wait, so we had our dinner. Afterwards, I took my gun and left the house to look for Uncle Reuben. It was very difficult to find my way in the thick mist. I called my uncle's name and searched among the bushes, but I could not find him. I had decided to return home when I heard a man's voice in the mist.

'God help me and forgive me!' said the voice.

I went towards the sound and found a small horse with a man on its back. He was tied to the horse. His feet were by the horse's neck and his head was near its tail. The little horse was frightened by this strange way of riding, and it was jumping around, trying to throw him off. The man was my Uncle Reuben, and he was nearly dead from fear.

I took him off the horse, put him on mine and led him to my home. He fell asleep as we went, and slept until we arrived. When we got home, he shook the water off his clothes and then went to sleep again. When he woke up, my mother and Annie fed him until he could eat nothing more, and they asked him many questions about his terrible adventure.

My uncle told us that the Doones had robbed him and taken his horse. Then they had tied him to the wild horse, saying, 'We want to have some fun.' For two or three hours they had chased the horse through the mist and laughed at his screams. Then they had become hungry and left him.

In the evening, Farmer Snowe, the head man of the village, came to visit us with his three daughters. Uncle Reuben sat

His feet were by the horse's neck and his head was near its tail.

quietly in the corner and did not say much, but at the end of the evening he spoke to Farmer Snowe about the Doones.

'You farmers are all afraid of the Doones,' he said. 'Why don't you all join together and chase the Doones out of their valley? You eat well and you talk well, but I think you're afraid to fight.'

◆

The next day, Uncle Reuben took me with him to visit the chief judge in this part of the country, Lord Wichehalse.

Lord Wichehalse greeted us in a very friendly way. He laughed when he heard Uncle Reuben's story.

'How are you so sure that those men were the Doones?' he asked. 'You say that there was a very thick mist. Could you see the men? Can you prove who they were?'

It was clear that the judge did not want to help, and when Uncle Reuben realized this, he became very angry.

'This isn't right!' he shouted. 'You can't allow it to continue! I'll go to London myself, and tell the king what's happening in Somerset.'

'Oh,' said Lord Wichehalse, 'so this happened in Somerset? But I'm only responsible for the king's peace in the county of Devon. Sir, you must go to the judge in Somerset.'

Uncle Reuben was still feeling very angry when we left Lord Wichehalse.

'Remember my words, John Ridd,' he said. 'I'm not going to forget this. I have a plan. I know an important man in London called Judge Jeffreys. He's the most important judge in the country. I'm going to send him a letter about the Doones.'

On our way home we saw some lovely spring flowers.

'Pretty flowers, aren't they?' said Uncle Reuben.

The flowers made me think of Lorna Doone. I thought of that day, long ago, when I met her. 'Does she ever think of me?' I wondered sadly.

A few days later, Uncle Reuben asked me to guide him to the Doone valley. We did not tell anybody where we were going. We rode through the Bagworthy forest to the hills that surrounded the valley. Then we climbed slowly and with difficulty to the top of a high hill. From there, we looked down. Uncle Reuben also looked at the hills around the valley.

'If they put big guns on top of the hills, soldiers could easily take this place,' he said. 'With three cannons on top of that hill there, and three cannons on top of this hill, we could destroy them.'

I was not listening to him. I was looking down into the valley at the little opening in the rock that I had once come through. As I looked at it, I saw someone pass close by it – someone white and small, and beautiful. It was Lorna Doone.

I could feel my heart beating. Seven years had passed, and I was a man now. I was sure that she had forgotten me, and I had half forgotten her. It was very strange, but at that moment I felt certain that my life was joined with hers.

Chapter 5   Return to the Valley

Soon after Uncle Reuben went home, I decided to visit the Doone valley again. I put on expensive new clothes, forgetting about the effect of water on them. I wanted to look my best. I walked to the waterfall that I had once climbed up. I was a big man now, and the whirlpool and the rocks seemed smaller than I remembered. I climbed up behind the waterfall, as I had done before, and I soon reached the top.

I hid behind the rock and looked out. Spring was very early that year. Already there were fresh young leaves on the trees and

18

small yellow flowers in the grass. The sky was very blue and the birds were singing sweet love songs.

Then I heard a sweet voice, sweeter than all the birds. It was the voice of Lorna Doone. I stayed behind the rocks, because I was afraid that the sweet singer would see me and run away. After a few minutes I looked out and saw her coming towards me, walking by the side of the stream. I could not see her face clearly. I saw only that her lovely dark hair had white flowers in it. It was sunset, and the soft light over the western hills made shadows behind her. Even now, when I see the sunset, I think of her on that day.

I came out from behind the rocks, and she turned to run away. I fell down on the grass, as I had fallen seven years ago when I reached the top of the waterfall.

'Lorna Doone,' I said. She turned round and smiled. I knew that she had recognized me, but she pretended to be angry.

'Who are you, sir?' she cried. 'And how do you know my name?'

'I'm John Ridd,' I answered. 'The boy who climbed up the waterfall seven years ago.'

'Yes, I remember. You were so frightened, and hid here in the water. But you've forgotten how dangerous this place is.'

I saw that she was afraid for me. Her soft, bright eyes watched me as she spoke, and I could not answer her. I knew that I would love her all my life, but I did not think I was good enough for her. It would be better, I thought, if I left immediately.

'Miss Lorna, I'll go,' I said. 'I can see that you're afraid. I know you'd be sad if they killed me. Try to think of me sometimes. I'll come again, and bring you some fresh eggs from our hens.'

'Thank you very much,' she said, 'but you mustn't come to look for me. You can leave the eggs in the hole in the rocks that I showed you.'

Then she smiled, and I wanted so much to find the way to her heart. She held her hand out to me and I touched it softly, then turned and climbed back down the rock.

All that week I dreamed of Lorna Doone. I could not work for very long at anything, and everybody thought I was ill. Our servant, John Fry, told people that a mad dog had bitten me. My mother almost believed him. In the evening she sat beside me and asked me questions that I did not want to answer. I only wanted to sit by the fire and think of Lorna Doone.

Chapter 6   Lorna's Story

I could not decide when to return to the Doone valley. I did not like hiding from people. And did Lorna think that I was just a stupid farmboy? But after some weeks, the weather became warm and sunny, and the hillsides were bright with flowers. I sat out under an old tree and cut the letters LD into it. Then I put on my good clothes, went into the Bagworthy forest and walked up the stream.

It had rained a lot the night before, and the waterfall was very full. The rock was difficult to climb, and I was tired when I reached the top. I crossed the little stream, then sat down to rest. After a few minutes I fell asleep.

◆

I woke when a shadow passed over me. It was early evening, and Lorna Doone was standing between me and the sun.

'John Ridd, are you mad?' she said, taking my hand to pull me up.

'Not mad, but half asleep,' I answered, wanting to keep her hand in mine.

'Come away, come away, if you care for your life. The guards will be here soon. Be quick, John Ridd, and let me hide you.'

But I said, 'I won't move a step, unless you call me John.'

'Well, John, then – John Ridd, be quick if you want to save your life.'

Without another word, she led me to the hole in the rocks, and I remembered again how I had escaped through it seven years ago. There were some low, thick bushes beside it. Lorna pushed the bushes to one side and showed me a small, narrow path through the rocks.

I followed her as well as I could, but because of my great size I hit my knees and arms very often. We soon came to an open space inside the rock, a little room with high walls of rock all round it and the blue sky for the ceiling. Lorna had covered the rock floor with grass and flowers, and it looked very pretty.

'Where are the fresh eggs you promised me, John Ridd?' she asked.

She thought I had forgotten them, but I had them in my bag. I took them out one by one and laid twenty-four eggs on the floor.

'Count them,' I said to her.

Lorna looked at them in surprise and began to cry.

'How have I made you cry?' I asked anxiously. 'What have I done?'

'You haven't done anything,' she answered proudly. 'I just cry sometimes. You've been very kind – they're not kind to me here.'

Her tears embarrassed me and I said nothing. Lorna walked away from me. Then she turned, sat down and started to tell me about her life.

◆

'There are only two people here who help me,' she began. 'My grandfather, Sir Ensor Doone, and the Counsellor, who's the wisest of all the Doones. My grandfather is a proud old man. He seems to know what's right and what's wrong, but he doesn't want to think about it. He's kind to me, but to no one else. The Counsellor's very clever, but he only talks because he likes talking.

'I can't remember my father or mother. They say that my father was the eldest son of Sir Ensor Doone, and that he was the bravest and best of men. They call me "Queen" and tell me that one day the valley will be mine.

'It's beautiful and peaceful here in the valley, and perhaps I should be happy. But the men kill and steal and drink and talk roughly. I don't feel that I belong to the Doones, and I hate their way of life. No one helps me or teaches me what's right.'

Lorna started to cry again. I did not know how to help her, so I said nothing. After a few minutes, she continued her story.

'The Counsellor's son, Carver Doone, wants to marry me. He's the strongest and bravest of all the Doones, but he's also the roughest and the cruellest. I don't like him, but he may force me to marry him. He often offers me stolen jewels.'

She saw from my face that I had heard of Carver. When she told me his name, and that he wanted Lorna as his wife, my heart was filled with anger.

Lorna continued, 'I had an aunt, Aunt Sabina, who was very kind to me. But she died a year ago, and now I have no one I can talk to, except my little servant girl, Gwenny Carfax. She's a little girl that we found almost dying in the hills. Her father went away one day and never returned. She has no family, so now she lives with us. The poor girl is fat and ugly, so none of the men are interested in her. She can go where she likes, and the guards don't stop her.

'Gwenny is very patient and kind, and her example helps me. I often want to run away from this valley because I hate the Doones so much. But then I think of my grandfather and my love for him. He's very old, and I don't want him to die without a gentle hand beside him. He's the only reason I stay. Once, someone wanted to help me escape, but it ended terribly. The events of that day changed my life. I stopped being a child and learned about death and darkness.

'It happened a year ago, although it seems like ten years. I was going home from here when a young man stepped out from behind a tree. He was beautifully dressed in red and green clothes.

'"Cousin Lorna, my good cousin," he said, "I'm Lord Alan Brandir. My father was your mother's brother, and the government made him your guardian. He's very old now, so they've asked me to be your guardian. I've been ordered to take care of you until you're twenty-one."

'I was very surprised by this, because he looked so young. "You, my guardian!" I said, and laughed. "You don't look much older than I am!"

'"I'm almost nineteen," he said with a laugh. "If one of the Doones attacked me, I'd kill him easily."

'But to me, he looked so young and thin. I was afraid for his life here in this place.

'"Don't be angry," he said softly. "I've travelled a long way to find you. I know how dangerous the Doones are – I've known men like them in the hills of Scotland. I'm not afraid of them, so don't be afraid for me. Will you come with me and leave this place?"

'A storm was starting, and the sky was growing dark. There was lightning in the sky, and thunder. I started to feel very frightened, and thought of my grandfather. I loved him too much to leave him.

'"I can't go with you, Lord Alan Brandir," I said. "You're too young, and I don't want to leave without my grandfather's permission. Please leave immediately – it's dangerous here."

'He took my hand and kissed it. "Dear cousin," he said, "Give me one flower so I can remember you. Believe me – I'll come back again soon."

'"You will not!" cried a loud voice. Carver Doone jumped from behind a tree and seized Alan Brandir in his arms like a cat jumping on a mouse. The boy fought bravely, but Carver lifted him up like a child and carried him away into the darkness. I heard the sound of someone falling to the ground. There was no scream, but I knew what had happened. The poor boy had been killed.

'I was young then. Only a year has passed, but I feel ten years older. I've known great violence, and I've felt sad and alone since then. There's no happiness in this valley, only darkness and death.'

◆

When Lorna finished her story, it was getting late.

'You must go now,' she whispered. 'Wait a month before you return. It's too dangerous.'

'But you may need me before that,' I said.

She pointed to a large white stone. 'You can see that stone from the hill opposite. If I need you, I'll put a black cloth over the stone.'

She hurried away through the trees, and I climbed down the back of the waterfall.

Chapter 7   London

The month of waiting was near its end. Every day I climbed the hill above the valley to see if there was a black cloth over the stone. But Lorna gave me no sign that she needed help. I thought about her every day. I was only a farmer, and I was afraid that a rich young lord would take her from me.

Then one afternoon, five days before the end of the month, I had been to feed the horses. I was just going back into the house, when a man came to our gate.

He held something up in his hand and shouted at me, 'In the king's name, come here!'

I walked slowly towards him. I was not going to hurry when someone shouted at me like that.

'Is this Ridd's farm?' he asked.

'Yes, sir, it is,' I answered. 'Come in and we'll give you something to eat.'

He was a man of about forty years of age, with a hard face and small, quick eyes.

'I'm hungry,' he said, 'but I won't eat or drink until I've seen and touched John Ridd.'

'You have seen and touched him,' I said. 'I'm John Ridd.'

'You're a big man, John Ridd,' he said. 'My name's Jeremy Stickles, and I'm a servant at the courts of law in London. In the king's name, take this.'

He gave me a letter and I read it carefully. It ordered me to go to London and answer questions from the king's judges. The government did not think that this part of the country was safe, and they wanted information. They also wanted information about the Doones.

The letter told me to hurry to London, but I waited for five days, hoping for a sign from Lorna Doone. But no black cloth appeared on the white rock, so I left my home and travelled with Jeremy Stickles to London.

In those days, the journey to London was long and dangerous. It took us many days to get there, but we arrived safely. The streets of London were dirty and noisy and full of people, and I did not like the city. I liked the River Thames and the big church at Westminster, but nothing else.

I waited in London for two months, until I had spent nearly all my money. I often went to the law courts, but I found no one to help me. Then one day an officer came from a courtroom and ordered me to go there. I entered and stood in front of one of the most powerful men in England, Judge Jeffreys.

The room was not very large. At one end there were three

high seats where three men were sitting. In the middle was Judge Jeffreys, a big, strong man with angry eyes.

'Who are you?' asked the judge.

'My name's John Ridd,' I answered. 'I was called to London two months ago by Jeremy Stickles. I've waited here, and nothing has happened, and now I want to go home. I have no more money.'

'Haven't you been paid for the journey and for your costs in the city?' Judge Jeffreys asked.

'No, sir.'

He called his officer. 'Pay this man immediately. He can come back to me tomorrow.'

The next day I returned to the court, and the judge questioned me.

'You're a big man, John,' he said. 'I have some questions for you. In your part of the country, are there thieves who do a lot of harm to people?'

'Yes, sir.'

'Why doesn't Lord Wichehalse hang them all? That's what he should do. He's the judge in that part of the country. Or he could send the robbers to me and I'll hang them,' said Judge Jeffreys.

'These robbers are from a very good family. They're dangerous, violent men and their home in the hills is very well protected. I think Lord Wichehalse is afraid,' I answered.

'What's the name of these people?'

'They're the Doones of Bagworthy forest, sir. We think there are about forty of them, but that doesn't include the women and children.'

'Forty Doones!' cried the judge. 'Forty thieves! How long have they been there?'

'About thirty or forty years, sir,' I answered.

'Did you know that Lord Wichehalse was a friend of the Doones?' said the judge, fixing his eyes on me.

I was very surprised. The idea was new to me, but I thought that it could be true.

'John Ridd, your eyes tell me everything I need to know. I see that you had not thought of it. Now, have you ever seen a man called Tom Faggus?'

'Yes, sir,' I said, 'I've often seen him. He's my cousin.'

'Tom Faggus is a good man. I know he's a thief – yes – but he's a good man and loyal to King Charles. But I'm afraid that another judge – not me – will hang him. Tell him to change his name and his profession. Now, one other thing. In your part of the country, are people talking about a rebellion against our king?'

'No, sir,' I answered. 'We're all quiet, good men and we're loyal to our king.'

'That's good,' said the judge. 'I like you, John Ridd. Keep away from the Doones, and from Lord Wichehalse. Say nothing about what's happened here. I'll send a man to your part of the country to tell me how things are. Now go. I'll remember you.'

◆

I travelled back to Somerset alone and arrived home safely. My mother and sisters were very pleased with the presents that I had bought for them in London. That day, everyone on the farm came to see me – the men, their wives and their children. They all wanted to hear my stories about London.

But, more than anything else, I wanted to visit Lorna. Early the next morning, I climbed to the top of the hill that looked over the Doone valley. I looked towards the white stone and saw that it was covered with a black cloth!

I did not know how long the stone had been covered, but I did not wait another minute. I went up the stream to the waterfall and climbed up into the valley.

Birds were singing in the golden evening. The trees were bright in the light of the sunset. I waited. At last Lorna came, looking very small and beautiful in the shadows. I ran towards her, not thinking of the guards or the danger. She looked frightened.

'Are you in trouble?' I asked.

'Oh, yes,' she answered, 'but that was a long time ago – two months or more, sir.' She looked away from me, with a cold look in her eyes.

I felt very frightened. Perhaps another man had taken her from me. I tried to turn away and leave, but could not. I could not stop myself – I started to cry.

Lorna heard it and it told her everything. She came to me and held out her hands. Her bright eyes were full of kindness.

'John Ridd,' she whispered softly, 'I didn't want to make you sad.'

'You're the only person who can do that,' I answered. I could not look at her.

'Come away from this bright place. Come into the shadows,' said Lorna.

She led me to her secret place in the rocks. Now she knew my feelings for her. She could not look at me, but she could not look away either.

'Lorna, do you love me?' I managed to say.

'Yes, I like you very much,' she answered.

'But do you love me, Lorna, more than all the world?'

'No,' she said. 'I like you very much, when you don't talk wildly. I like your strength. You could even fight Carver and beat him – I like that. But I put the black cloth on the rock two months ago, and you didn't come. Why didn't you come when I needed help, if you like me so much? The Counsellor's trying to make me marry Carver. My grandfather thinks I'm too young – Carver's thirty-five and I'm only seventeen. Another man, Charlie Doone, watches me all the time too, so my grandfather's afraid that Carver and Charlie will fight because of me. People watch me and follow me everywhere I go. I'm only here with you today because little Gwenny Carfax helps me.'

When I heard this, I promised never to leave Lorna again. I gave her the little present that I had brought her from London. I explained why I had not come, and was forgiven. We spoke sweet words to each other. Her eyes and her words showed me that she had begun to care for me, and I was happier than I had ever been. We planned how she could send news to me if she needed me.

'Now go, John,' she said. 'You must go home. You can come and see me again in two months.'

Then she turned and ran down the valley.

Chapter 8   Friends and Enemies

At this time, we began to hear strange stories in the village. King Charles II had no children, and he wanted his brother, James, to be king after his death. People said that some men in this part of the country were against James and were preparing to fight against him. When I heard this, I remembered Judge Jeffreys's words. I said nothing, but I was afraid of what might happen.

One evening I had a long talk with Annie. I knew that she was in love with Tom Faggus. She hoped that he would ask her to marry him.

'Be careful,' I said. 'Tom's a highwayman!'

'And what are the Doones?' Annie said. 'Aren't they highwaymen, too? But you love one of them.'

I was very surprised. 'How did you know?' I asked.

'I didn't know,' she answered. 'I only guessed it from some things you've said. And I knew that you went to the Doone valley to see someone. Now I know it's true.'

I told Annie all about my love for Lorna, but I did not tell my mother, because the Doones had killed my father. I was afraid she would be very angry.

◆

On my last visit to Lorna, I had promised not to go to the valley for two months. When the eight weeks ended, I climbed up there again. But although I waited until the moon came up, Lorna did not come.

I went again the next day with a present of fish and eggs, which I put in a little bed of grass near the edge of the water. As I was putting them there, I saw a man coming slowly down the valley. I quickly hid behind a tree. The man came nearer, and I saw that his face was cold and cruel.

He came to the edge of the water and saw the eggs and fish.

'So!' he cried angrily, 'Charlie's leaving presents here for Lorna!'

The man's face became black with anger, and I guessed that he was Carver Doone. This was the man who wanted to marry Lorna! He took the fish and the eggs and went away. I waited, but Lorna did not come. All the beauty of the evening had gone.

◆

The next day I went to the valley again, and waited near the entrance to Lorna's secret place. Suddenly there was the sound of a gun. The shot went through my hat and carried it off my head. The hat fell into the water and was carried away over the waterfall. Shaking with fear, I quickly hid behind a rock.

Carver came out from behind some bushes and ran to the edge of the waterfall. He stood within a few feet of where I was hiding.

'Have I killed you, Charlie?' he shouted. 'This is the third time that I've shot at you.'

He went away laughing, and I laughed too – silently. I felt sure that one day I would fight Carver Doone and win Lorna from him.

That evening, our servant, Betty, made strange signs to me, then came and whispered in my ear, 'Lorna Doone'. I quickly followed her out of the house.

When we got outside she said, 'I have a message for you from Lorna Doone. Her servant brought it. Lorna can't meet you in the evenings. Go to the valley in the morning.'

◆

Of course, I was up the next morning before the October sunrise. I climbed up into the valley while the first light of morning was coming over the hills. Winter was near, and the trees and bushes were touched with red and gold. At last I stood at the top of the rock. I looked up the valley and saw Lorna. She looked glad to see me, and this made me happy.

'At last you've come, John!' she cried. 'They've kept me prisoner in my house every evening.'

I followed her into her hiding-place in the rocks. Lorna started to speak of the difficulties and dangers of her life, but I said softly, 'That isn't what I want to hear.'

'What do you mean?' she said, pretending not to understand me.

'Do you love me?' I asked.

'I love you,' she said. 'But how does that help us? My life is too dangerous. We can never marry. It can never happen – never.'

I went home that day feeling happy and sad. When I got home, I found Tom Faggus there; he had come to tell my mother that he wanted to marry Annie.

That same day, I told my mother about Lorna. She understood and accepted my feelings, and that made me very happy.

Chapter 9   Danger in the Valley

One afternoon, Jeremy Stickles arrived at our house. He led me into a field and looked carefully around to see that no one was listening.

'John,' he said, 'Judge Jeffreys spoke to you about the possibility of a rebellion in this part of the country. That's why I've come here. We know that the Duke of Monmouth is looking for men to fight against the king's brother, James. I've been sent to discover more about this plan. You may be ordered to fight for the king.'

◆

Several weeks passed. Each day Lorna left a sign to tell me that she was safe. But suddenly these signs ended, and I was very frightened for her. Each day my fear grew.

Three times I went into the valley and waited for her, but she did not come. Once I followed the stream far up the valley and came to a small stone house. I guessed it was the house of Carver Doone and listened carefully, but there was no one inside. Before I went home that night, I decided that I would enter the valley again from the other end. I wanted to discover where they kept Lorna.

The next day, I went on foot round the hills to the southern entrance to the Doone valley. It was nearly dark when I got there. Just as I arrived at the entrance, the moon came out. I stepped back quickly into the shadows.

A heavy tree hung over the entrance to the valley. The Doones could let it fall if an enemy tried to go in. I call it an 'entrance', but there were three entrances into the valley and only the Doones knew which was the right one. They often changed it, and if you chose the wrong one, you would die.

I guessed, and chose the middle opening. I went in and was

soon in total darkness. I fell over something hard and long – a cannon. This made me think that I had come the right way.

As I turned the next corner, I saw two Doones guarding the path into the valley. I hid quickly and watched them for some time. Their lamp was on the ground and they were playing a game, but each man held a gun in his hand. I heard them call each other by their names. One of the men was Charlie Doone and the other was called Phelps. They began to argue, and Charlie threw his glass in Phelps's face. The glass fell, hit the lamp and broke it.

'Go and get another lamp from Carver's house,' Phelps said angrily.

Charlie got up and walked in my direction, singing strangely to himself. He passed very close to me as I stood deep in the shadows, and his coat touched my hand. I followed him as he turned this way and that way, and at last I came to open sky and saw all the houses of the Doones spread out below me.

Charlie continued walking and I followed, keeping in the shadows. He stopped at an open door. Carver was standing just inside.

'What do you want at this time of night?' he asked.

'I want a new lamp. The other fell and broke,' said Charlie.

I did not stop, but continued walking to the next house. Suddenly a watchman came towards me in the darkness.

'Who are you? Answer or I'll shoot!' he shouted.

His gun was pointing at me. I was very frightened but I began to sing. I wanted the man to think I was a Doone, so I sang the little song that Charlie had sung.

When the man heard it, he said, 'All right,' then went away. I learned afterwards that the song was the secret song of Carver Doone. The guard had thought that I was him.

A face appeared at a window. It was Lorna, looking to see who had shouted. Her face was very sad.

'Lorna, it's me,' I whispered.

'Oh, John!' she whispered, 'you must be mad to come here!'

'I had to come, you know that,' I replied. 'You knew I would come. What's happened? Why hasn't there been any sign from you? Are you in danger?'

'My grandfather, Sir Ensor, is very ill,' she replied. 'I'm afraid he won't live long. Counsellor and Carver Doone control the valley now, and I don't dare go outside the house. I'm frightened that Carver will seize me. Gwenny, my servant, isn't allowed to leave the valley.'

'How can I know if you're in danger? You must make some sign to me.'

Lorna thought for a time, then said, 'Do you see that high tree with seven birds' nests in it? You can see it from outside the valley. Gwenny can climb up that tree. She'll take away one of the nests if there's danger. If you can only see six nests in the tree, you'll know that I'm in trouble. If you can only see five nests, you'll know that Carver has carried me away.'

'Oh, God!' I said, and the anger in my voice frightened Lorna.

'Don't worry,' she whispered sadly. 'I won't let him touch me. If I have to, I'll kill myself.'

I only said, 'God protect you.' She said the same to me, in a low, sad voice. We said a sweet goodbye to each other, and I went home.

◆

Jeremy was staying with us and acting very strangely. He went out every morning and came back late at night, and no one knew where he went or what he did.

One morning, Tom Faggus came to our house to see Annie. I went out alone, thinking of my love for Lorna. It was so easy for Tom and Annie, and so difficult for me! I went to the little wood near our house and began to cut wood for the fires.

Near the wood there was a little stream, with bushes growing along its edge. As I was working there, three men came very quietly down the other side of the stream. I saw that they were Doones! I lay down in the grass and hid. The men stopped. One of them looked over the top of the bushes and said, 'Someone has been working here, cutting wood.'

It was Carver Doone who spoke. Charlie Doone was with him and, to my great surprise, I recognized Lord Wichehalse. Why was he with them?

'There's no one here,' said Charlie. 'We can hide here. It's near the path that Jeremy Stickles comes along every morning.'

'We'll wait for him here,' said Lord Wichehalse. 'It will be his last journey.'

So Lord Wichehalse was working with the Doones against the king! And they had come to kill Jeremy Stickles! I had to warn him! Perhaps he had already left the farm and was walking towards the wood! I left the wood quietly, and then began to run. Suddenly a gun was pressed against my side.

'Oh!' said Jeremy. 'It's you!' He put down the gun. 'Why are you running?' he asked.

'I've come to warn you. Two of the Doones and Lord Wichehalse are in the wood there, with long guns. They're waiting for you.'

Jeremy was a brave man, but he started shaking when he heard this.

'I know they've been watching me. That's why I pointed my gun at you, John,' he said. He thought for a moment, then said slowly, 'Let them wait. I can't bring soldiers to catch them, and three Doones are too many for you and me. You don't even have a gun. So let them wait. This only means that we must fight the Doones in their valley sooner than I expected.'

◆

It was Carver Doone who spoke.

The next day, Jeremy led me outside the house. He told me that he had discovered more about the possible rebellion against the king's brother. He was now certain that many people in this part of the country hated James. Most of these people were young and not very wise, but some of the great lords in the area were leading them. The Doones and Lord Wichehalse were among the leaders. The government wanted Jeremy to discover more about their plans. Jeremy was also making plans for soldiers to move the Doones out of their valley.

'We'll kill them if necessary,' he said.

'Kill all the Doones!' I cried. 'That would be terrible!' I was thinking of Lorna.

'Do you like it when the Doones steal your cows and your money?' Jeremy asked. 'You should be glad to hear this!'

'I won't help! I won't fight!' I said.

'You won't fight against the men who killed your father! Your Uncle Reuben is with us, you know. He's promised to lead our soldiers against the Doone valley.'

But I was afraid for Lorna. If the soldiers caught her, what would happen? What should I do?

Chapter 10   Escape

In the middle of December, the weather became very cold. Snow fell. I went out to look at the tree with the nests that Lorna was using as a sign. I looked at them – and looked again. I could only see six nests! Lorna needed me!

Then I saw Gwenny, Lorna's servant, coming over the snow.

'Come with me,' she said. 'Sir Ensor's dying. He knows about you. He wants to see you before he dies.'

I went with Gwenny to the valley, entering by a secret path that I had never seen before. We passed two Doones, who stared at me, but Gwenny said something and they allowed me to pass. At last we came to the door of Sir Ensor's house. I went inside and Lorna met me.

'Don't be afraid of him,' she said.

She led me to a cold, dark room and went away. Sir Ensor was sitting up in bed. He was still a handsome man, but there was death in his proud old face. His white hair fell to his shoulders, and his pale fingers were lying on his knees without moving. Only his great black eyes seemed to be alive. They were fixed on me.

'Are you John Ridd?' he said slowly.

'John Ridd is my name, sir. I hope you're better.'

'Boy, do you know what you've been doing? How can you, a farmer, want to marry Lorna Doone? Do you know that she comes from one of the oldest families in Europe?' he said.

'I didn't know that. But I knew that the Doones were a good family,' I answered. 'The Ridds have been honest farmers for hundreds of years. We've been farmers much longer than the Doones have been thieves.'

I expected the old man to be angry, but he spoke quietly. 'Will you promise never to see Lorna again, never to speak to her again? Call her!'

I went and found Lorna. We entered the room hand in hand, and Sir Ensor looked very surprised. For forty years he had been obeyed and feared by everyone around him.

'You two fools!' he said. 'You two fools!'

'Sir, perhaps we're not as stupid as we look,' I said quietly. 'But if we *are* fools, we'll be happy fools. We only want to be together.'

He was silent for some time, just looking at us.

'Well, John,' he said finally, and his eyes smiled, 'I can see you're not a complete fool.'

'Oh, no, Grandfather!' cried Lorna. 'Nobody knows how clever John is. Nobody except me!' Then she turned and kissed me.

I felt very embarrassed by this, and Lord Ensor's eyes opened wide.

'I've seen a little of the world,' he said, 'but nothing like this. People do this kind of thing in southern climates, not in the mists of Exmoor.'

'We love each other, sir,' I said. 'It happens all over the world.'

He did not reply, but I think he understood our love. He coughed a little, and when he spoke at last, he sounded very tired.

'You're fools, so be fools together,' he said. 'Be boy and girl until you have grandchildren. It's the best thing I can wish you.'

His eyes closed, and suddenly he looked very ill. His hand went down into the bed and I saw that he was feeling for something. I put my hand into the bed and felt something hard. I pulled out a necklace and a ring and gave them to him. He called Lorna to the bed and put them in her hands.

'Oh!' said Lorna, 'It's the glass necklace and ring he always promised me.' She gave them to me. 'The necklace will be safer with you,' she said. 'And put the ring on your finger.'

I did as she asked. We stayed by Lord Ensor's bedside and he died peacefully that same day. He did not ask for anyone to come to him, not even the Counsellor. Only Lorna wept for him. He had been a cold, angry man, and no one except Lorna had loved him.

◆

The new year came, and more snow fell. It stopped the rivers and covered the roads. It came up as high as the windows, and we were forced to dig our way out of the farmhouse. Many of our animals were lost, and we had to go out and save them.

It was very difficult to walk in the snow because it was so soft. Annie, who read a lot of books, told me that in cold countries men made things called 'snowshoes'. I made some snowshoes for myself. It was difficult to walk in them but I practised hard, and after some days I was able to move across the snow quite fast.

Late in January, I went to the top of the hill and looked out over the Doone valley. Everything was covered with snow. Then I began to think that perhaps poor Lorna was cold and unable to leave her house. I did not think that the Doones would be outside in this weather; surely it was safe to go to her.

I left the farm and walked to Lorna's house. When I got there, I knocked quietly on the door.

'Who is it?' asked Gwenny from inside.

'John Ridd,' I answered.

'Put your finger through the hole in the door and show me your ring,' she said. 'And if you're not John Ridd, I'll cut your finger off!'

I laughed and showed my finger.

'What's the meaning of this, Gwenny?' I asked.

'They've shut us in and we have no food. We're very hungry! I could eat you. I could eat anything!'

I had brought food with me. I passed some bread through a little opening above the door. Gwenny seized it and I watched through the hole as she ate it like an animal. I could see Lorna lying in a chair, so I passed in water and bread for her and she began to eat. Then she came to the door.

'I didn't expect to see you again,' she whispered through the hole. 'I expected to die. Carver has shut us in here. He says I can't leave this house until I marry him.'

I gave her the rest of the food that I had brought. While the two girls ate, I stayed and talked to them.

Then Lorna said, 'Turn round and look up the valley. Soon they'll light the great fire. They've made Carver Captain of the Doones. There's going to be a big celebration. They'll eat and drink all night.'

When Lorna told me this, I thought, 'The fire will fill the valley with light and they might see me.' But then I thought,

'No, if the Doones are eating and drinking tonight, they won't watch the valley. It will be quite safe.'

'Lorna, I'll be back again in two hours,' I said. 'Just pack a few things. I'll come back and break down the door. Then I'll take you and Gwenny to my home.'

◆

I went home as quickly as possible and told my mother to make the house warm. My sister Annie gave me a coat for Lorna. Then I left the house again and made the journey to the valley.

I came to Lorna's house and called, but there was no answer. The door was open, and in the middle of the room I saw Gwenny Carfax on the floor, holding on to a man by his foot. Lorna was in a corner, holding a chair between herself and another man. This man was trying to pull the chair away and reach her.

I ran inside, picked the first man – Charlie Doone – up off the floor and threw him out of the window. Then I carried the second man – Lord Wichehalse – out of the door and threw him into the deep snow. I took Lorna and Gwenny outside and put Annie's warm coat round both of them. Then we started the long, hard journey over the snow to the farm.

When we got home, my mother came out and kissed Lorna. We brought her and Gwenny into the house and Mother put Lorna in a big chair, where she lay with her eyes closed, her hand in mine.

Chapter 11   The Necklace

A month later, it was possible to travel again, and Tom Faggus came to visit Annie. He was not a highwayman now; he had bought some land and become a farmer.

I told him the story of Lorna, and of my discussion with Sir Ensor on his deathbed. Then I showed him the necklace.

'It's only glass,' I said.

Tom took it to the window and examined it carefully. 'Glass!' he cried. 'This necklace is made of the finest diamonds. You could sell them for more money than your whole farm!'

He had the necklace in his hands when Lorna came in.

'How much money will you take for this?' he asked. 'Will you take five pounds?'

'It's pretty,' said Lorna, 'but five pounds is too much – and I don't want to sell it. My grandfather gave it to me.'

'If this was sold in London,' said Tom, 'you'd get a hundred thousand pounds.'

Lorna did not say much when she heard this, but I knew what she was thinking. She thought that the Doones had stolen it from a great lady. We did not talk about it, and Lorna did not wear it. Instead, she put it away in a corner of the house.

◆

Tom Faggus left the next day, and several hours later, Jeremy Stickles came in, covered in mud from head to foot. He told us that three Doones had tried to kill him. They had shot one of the soldiers who was with him.

The snow was deep on the ground. In this cold weather, I knew that the Doones would not attack the farm and try to take Lorna back. But they would come when the snow had gone. I was sorry that Tom Faggus had left, because he was a useful man and a good fighter.

I discussed the problem with Jeremy.

'Call all the men you know,' he said. 'You'll need them to help you fight the Doones.'

The next day, I rode out to find Jeremy Stickles's soldiers. I found only four, but told them to come to the farm as quickly as possible. They promised to bring two more men with them. Then I rode back as quickly as possible. It was fortunate that I did this, because something terrible had happened.

Lorna had gone out into the garden. Just as she was returning to the house, she saw two eyes looking at her from the bushes. It was Carver Doone! She stood there, too frightened to move or speak. Carver laughed, lifted his gun and pointed it at Lorna's heart. She still could not move. He slowly pointed the gun down at the ground. Then he fired, and earth was thrown up all over Lorna. She fell to the ground and wept. Carver came closer to her.

'I haven't killed you this time,' he said, 'because I never kill in anger. But I will kill you, unless you come back to the Doone valley tomorrow. You must bring back the things that you took away. And I will kill John Ridd.'

Then he turned and left.

◆

We made our preparations. We brought a lot of food into the house, and the four soldiers and their two friends stayed at the farm with us. We sent all the women away except Gwenny and our old servant, Betty. There had been heavy rain, and water covered the land in the Doone valley. Because of this, we thought that only eight or ten men would attack us. We had eight men with guns and four others with sticks and knives.

I hoped that I would meet Carver Doone, because I wanted to kill him with my own hands. I was big and strong, and no man had ever beaten me in a fight. But Carver was as big and strong as I was. I knew he would be my equal in a fight.

Each day, Gwenny climbed up into a tall tree to watch for the Doones. One afternoon, in the middle of March, she came running to me. 'The Doones are coming!' she cried.

She went to tell Jeremy Stickles and his men. Soon, the Doones arrived at the back of the farmhouse. They did not know that our men and I were waiting in the shadow of the house.

'We'll burn the house down,' said the deep voice of Carver Doone. 'But if one of you hurts Lorna, I'll kill you. She belongs to me.'

I had my gun in my hands and I pointed it at Carver, but my hands did not move. Why didn't I shoot him? I had never killed a man before, and I could not do it.

Two of the Doones came towards the house, carrying burning branches. They were unable to see me because of the smoke. I ran out, struck one man and broke his arm. With a cry of pain he dropped the branch. The other man stopped, and I threw the burning branch into his face. When he jumped at me, I caught him and broke his shoulder. Then I threw him down on the first man.

There was a loud noise. The soldiers had fired and two robbers fell. I ran to Carver and seized his beard.

'Do you call yourself a man?' I shouted. He tried to point his gun at me, but I was too quick for him. 'Now, Carver,' I said, 'be careful! I may not be very clever, but I'm as big as you are. Down! Down into the dust!'

I threw him on his back, and when the other men saw this they ran away. They left their horses and the two dead men. One man fired his gun at me as he ran, and hit me in the leg. I fell, and Carver got to his feet and ran after the others.

The wound in my leg frightened the women, of course, but it was very small and did not hurt much.

◆

Soon after this, more soldiers arrived, so we did not fear another attack by the Doones. Then one evening, when I was coming home from the fields, my sister Lizzie met me.

'There's a big man here, very fat, with wild white hair. I think he's a Doone,' she said.

'I think I know who it is. It must be the Counsellor!' I replied.

I found Lorna, and together we went to my mother's room. Mother was standing at the door of the room, talking to the Counsellor.

He held out his hands to Lorna. 'My dear child,' he said, 'how well you look. Kiss your uncle.'

'You smell of smoke,' Lorna said. 'I don't want to kiss you.'

'You're right, my child,' he said, and laughed. He turned to me. 'So this is John Ridd, the brave man who wants to marry our Lorna? Her father was the eldest son of Sir Ensor. I'm the second son. As Lorna's guardian, I agree to this marriage. I'm sure you'll be happy together.'

'Oh, you are very kind, sir!' my mother said.

'They'll be a fine couple,' said the Counsellor. 'We hope that John will join us in the valley.'

'Oh, no, sir, oh, no!' cried Mother. 'You really mustn't think of it. John's an honest man!'

'Yes, well, we certainly don't want honest men. Don't you think he might change?'

'Oh, no, sir, never!

'All right,' said the Counsellor. 'But Lorna, I think you should thank me. I've agreed to the marriage.'

Lorna looked into her uncle's eyes. 'I don't think you've agreed because you love me. I think you want something from me.'

'My dear, I only want your happiness.'

After this discussion, I led the Counsellor into the kitchen and gave him food and a bed for the night.

After the second glass of beer, he said to me, 'You're good people. You don't give me up to the soldiers – you just try to make me drunk!'

The next morning, Lorna told me that she had heard someone walking around the house during the night.

'I think the Counsellor was looking for something,' she said.

When Annie went outside to milk the cows, the Counsellor followed her.

'Did you know that if you pass a glass necklace over milk, the milk will be creamier?' he said.

'No,' said Annie, 'I've never heard that.'

'Have you got a glass necklace?' asked the Counsellor.

'Lorna has one,' said Annie. 'I know where it is. I'll go and get it.'

She ran off and got the necklace. The Counsellor passed the necklace over the milk, and then put it under the milk pot.

'Leave it here under the milk pot for a day and a night,' he said, 'and don't tell anyone about it.'

'All right, I'll do that,' said Annie, and went back into the house.

A few minutes later, the Counsellor politely said goodbye to my mother. Then he left the farm, taking Lorna's necklace with him.

Chapter 12   Jeremy's Story

That same night, Jeremy Stickles told me that everything was ready for the great battle against the Doones. I told him how the Counsellor had stolen the necklace.

'I know something about that necklace,' Jeremy said. 'I was in Watchet a few days ago, and I met an Italian woman called Benita. She used to be a servant to a rich English lord and his family in Italy. The English lord often talked to Benita about his family. He told her that one member of his family had lost all his lands and become an outlaw.

'Sadly, the English lord was killed when he was out riding one day. His wife took her little daughter and Benita with her to England. The family house was in this part of the country and they travelled here in a carriage. The lady knew about the Doones, but wasn't afraid of them. "Highwaymen don't rob ladies and their children," she said.

'They passed the little town of Watchet and were near the sea, when they saw horsemen riding towards them. The driver of the carriage tried to drive faster, but the carriage stopped in the soft sand. As the horsemen came closer to the carriage, the lady was able to see their faces. "I know one of those men," she cried. "He's the member of our family who became an outlaw."

'Benita was carrying the box of family jewels. There was a diamond necklace in it, and she put it round the neck of the little girl. Then the highwaymen pushed the carriage over on its side. After that, Benita remembers nothing. When she opened her eyes, the Doones had gone, taking the little girl. The lady was carried to the town of Watchet, but she died soon after that.

'Benita stayed in that part of the country. She had no money, because the Doones had taken everything. The lady's lands are under the protection of the government. If they ever find the owner, they'll return the lands to her.'

'I suppose,' I said, 'that the owner is the little girl who was carried away by the Doones.'

'Yes.'

I remembered the day, long ago, when I was riding home from school. I remembered the foreign servant who asked me for a glass of water. I remembered how we passed the carriage with the lady and the little girl in it. And I remembered how we saw the Doones, riding across the moor with a little girl.

It was very clear. Lorna belonged to a great family of lords, and she was the owner of great lands. She was too good for me; perhaps I could never marry her.

I rode to Watchet and met Benita. I showed her the old ring that Sir Ensor had given Lorna. Benita recognized it immediately as the lady's ring.

Lorna was not a Doone; her real name was Dugal. She was the daughter of Lord Dugal, and I now understood the Doones' plan. They wanted Carver to marry Lorna because then they would get all her land.

Chapter 13   The Battle of the Valley

Jeremy Stickles had a plan for the great attack on the Doones in their valley. He had 155 men and three small cannons. Thirty-five of the men were from the king's own guards, and they had horses. There were also horses to pull the cannons. Then there were sixty men from Somerset and sixty men from Devon who were not soldiers and had no horses.

The plan was that the Somerset men, with one cannon, would attack from the eastern hills. The Devon men, with the second cannon, would attack from the west. Jeremy Stickles and I took thirty-five men and one cannon. We intended to attack through the southern entrance to the Doone valley. That was our plan. But things did not happen as we had intended.

◆

We reached the Doone gate and started to prepare the cannon. As we had hoped, we heard the noise of shooting from the east and the west. Suddenly, ten or twelve guns fired at us, and several of our men fell.

Jeremy and I were at the front, and the cannon was pulled behind us by some of my own horses. We saw that the enemy were hidden in some bushes, and we ran forward to fight them.

Suddenly there was a loud noise behind us and a terrible cry from the men and the horses. A great tree had been dropped down from the top of the hill onto the horses and the cannon. It had fallen on two men and had broken the back of one of the horses and the leg of another.

I loved these horses, and this made me wild with anger. I ran towards the place where the tree had fallen. Then I saw Jeremy. He was lying on the ground with a wounded leg, unable to move. I picked him up and carried him to a safer place.

A boy came running towards me. 'We've lost the battle!' he cried. 'The men of Devon and Somerset are fighting each other. The Doones have beaten us!'

Later, I discovered why these men had fought against each other. When the Devon men reached the top of the western hill, they prepared their cannon. Then, without aiming the gun, they fired. The shot flew across the valley and hit the Somerset men on the other side, killing two men.

Of course, the Somerset men were very angry. They aimed their gun at the Devon men and fired. Four or five men fell. Then a battle began between the two groups. Suddenly, the Doones appeared – they had come up a secret path. They attacked the Somerset men, killed four and took their cannon. The Devon men pulled their cannon home, and that was the end of the battle.

◆

Jeremy Stickles was very ill for several weeks, but he slowly got better. In May, Annie and Tom Faggus got married and moved to his farm, which was not far from ours.

Because Jeremy Stickles was still weak, I went away for some months to do government work for him. When I returned to the farm, Lorna did not come out to meet me.

'Where's Lorna?' I asked.

'Lady Lorna Dugal has gone to London,' said Lizzie. 'I don't think she'll come back again.'

'What? Has she gone?' I cried wildly. 'Has Lorna gone? She never said goodbye to me!'

'She wept, but she had to go,' Lizzie said. 'She left a letter for you. It's in her room.'

I ran to Lorna's room and found the letter.

My Dear One,

I have to leave and cannot even say goodbye to you. The men will not wait. My uncle, a great lord, is waiting for me at Dunster. The king has ordered him to take care of me until I am twenty-one years old. It is very cruel. I said that I did not want my lands or my money; I only wanted to stay here. But they told me that I have to obey the king's order. Nothing will ever take me away from you. I will always be your own Lorna Dugal.

'It has all ended,' I thought. But my heart answered sweetly, 'No, you'll be happy again.'

Chapter 14   The Search for Tom Faggus

For many months I received no letters from Lorna. I did not know where to write to her, and I began to think that she had forgotten me. But I often heard news of her. Travellers from London told us that Lorna was already famous for her beauty. Many young lords wanted to marry her for her money. I felt very sad, and was sure I had lost her. I could never forget her but I tried to work hard on the farm.

The new year came. In February 1685 we received the news that King Charles II had died. His brother, James II, was now King of England. We heard too that the Duke of Monmouth was coming from France to the south of England. Many farmers in the south wanted to join him in a rebellion against the new king. There was talk that Judge Jeffreys was coming to hang the rebels.

◆

Some months later, Annie came to see me, weeping.

'Oh, John,' she said, 'Tom has gone with the Duke of Monmouth's rebels to fight against King James! Please find him and bring him back!'

'I'll try, I promise,' I said.

Next day, I rode out to look for Tom. At last, I found the Duke's soldiers at Bridgwater. They were not real soldiers, only countrymen who had not been taught to fight or use a gun.

I was very tired and stayed the night in a pub. The lady of the house woke me very early in the morning.

'The battle has begun,' she said.

I heard the sound of guns and dressed quickly. I rode out of town and onto the marshes, but there was a thick mist and it was difficult to see the way.

I came to a little village called Zeeland. The king's men had been there and their cooking fires were still burning, but the men were gone. I found a young man who knew the country and asked him to be my guide. He led me to the back of the Duke's army. It was four o'clock in the morning when we came out on the open marshes. The sun came up, and by its light I saw a terrible sight.

Men were flying in fear from a great battle, covered with blood and dust. Their only hope was to stay alive. Dead men lay on the ground with wide-open eyes. They were countrymen who had known nothing of war or battle; their hands had never held a gun. And here they lay dead and dying.

The men shouted to me as I passed them, 'The battle has ended! The cannons have come! They're killing us all!'

I tried to help some of the men, although I was almost in tears

51

at the sight of their pain. I gave some water to a dying man, who asked me to tell his wife about money hidden in an apple tree. Then I felt a soft touch on my face and looked up. Tom's horse, Winnie, looked at me, then turned her head. I realized that she was trying to tell me something. She ran away a few steps, then turned and looked at me again. I got on my horse and followed her.

We came near the front line of the battle. The Duke's men were standing beside a river that they could not cross. They had no guns, but shouted at the king's men on the other side, 'Come over and fight us!'

The king's soldiers lifted their guns and shot them down. Then the king's horsemen came at them from behind and rode in among them. I heard the noise of that fight, and the cries of the men who were struck down.

I followed Winnie for a long time until she stopped near a little hut. She made a low sound, and I realized she was calling to Tom. There was no answer, so she went inside.

Tom Faggus had been shot by the king's men and there was a great hole in his side. I gave him some water and he opened his eyes, then he put up his hand and touched Winnie.

'Is Winnie hurt?' he asked.

'No,' I said.

'Put me on her back,' he said.

I put him on Winnie's back and she went away. She seemed to know where to go, and soon they were out of sight.

I lay down in the hut and slept.

◆

I slept for three or four hours, and when I woke there were a lot of soldiers in the hut.

'What are you doing here?' they asked. 'You must be one of the Duke of Monmouth's rebels.'

'My name's John Ridd. I'm a farmer and I'm loyal to the king,' I said quickly.

'Oh, no, you're not. You're fighting for the Duke of Monmouth,' said an officer. 'Get up! We're going to hang you on that tree over there!'

I thought quickly. 'You'll have to catch me first,' I said. 'Put down your guns and fight me with your hands.'

They laughed at the thought that I wanted to fight so many men. The first man put down his gun and ran at me. I caught him by the back of his neck and threw him over the heads of his friends. The next soldier knew how to fight, but he was a small man and I threw him easily. The others were afraid, and stood talking to each other. I ran among them, throwing them to the left and right, then I jumped on my horse. They fired some shots after me, but I escaped.

Half an hour later, I was caught by another group of men. They stood across the road in front of me and made me get down from my horse.

'Here's another of the Duke's men!' they cried. 'A big one!'

They gave me no opportunity to speak. 'Hang him from that tree!' ordered an officer.

They put ropes round me and pulled me towards the tree. Two men were already hanging from it. Just then, a man came riding round the corner. It was Jeremy Stickles. He saw me and immediately realized what was happening. He rode over to the officer.

'Stop!' he cried. 'I know this man!' The two men talked together and I heard the words 'Judge Jeffreys' and 'London'.

The officer did not look very happy, but eventually he said, 'I'll leave him with you, then, Captain Stickles. The prisoner will be your responsibility.'

'John Ridd, you're my prisoner. Follow me,' Jeremy said loudly.

The first man put down his gun and ran at me.

The soldiers freed me, I climbed on my horse and I rode away behind Jeremy.

'Thank you, Jeremy Stickles,' I said. 'You saved my life.'

'You saved me from the Doones, John,' he said. 'Now we're equal again. But don't try to run away – the soldiers know your name. If you run away, your farm will be seized, and your mother and sisters will die of hunger. I'll take you to court in London. Here, they don't give you a chance to speak – they just hang you. But in London, the judge will listen.'

So we started on the journey to London. As we rode, I often thought of Lorna, and wondered if she still loved me.

Chapter 15   London Again

When I reached London, I heard that Lorna was living with her mother's uncle, Lord Brandir. I also heard that the queen liked Lorna very much, and that they often went to church together. I was not kept in prison, and could go where I wanted in the city. So I went to the church and waited among the crowd, hoping to see my Lorna.

The king and queen arrived, surrounded by many lords and great men. Then came beautiful ladies who were serving the queen. And then I saw Lorna. As I looked at her, she turned and saw me. Her eyes were very gentle and sweet as we looked at each other.

I went into the church and sat down. While I was sitting there, a man brought me a note from Lorna, telling me to visit her at her house the next day.

◆

Gwenny Carfax opened the door to Lord Brandir's house, and led me into a large room. After a few minutes, Lorna came in.

She was wearing a white dress and looked very lovely, but there was sadness in her face.

'Why haven't you replied to my letters?' she asked, and started to cry.

'Because you sent me none,' I answered.

'What?' cried Lorna, and she went and spoke to Gwenny.

At last I discovered why I had not received any letters from Lorna. The servant girl had hidden them because she wanted Lorna to marry a great lord. But Lorna told me that she hated London life.

'These important men only love me for my money,' she said. 'I only think of you. Come and see me often, John.'

◆

In the next weeks, while I was waiting to go to court, I often visited Lorna. One evening, as I was leaving Lord Brandir's house, I looked back and saw three men waiting in the shadows.

'What are those men doing there?' I thought. 'They must be thieves. I'll wait and see what their plan is.'

I hid in some bushes near the house. Soon, the lights in the house went out. Everybody had gone to bed. I heard a low call from some trees near the house, and the men walked quietly past me to an open window and climbed in. I went quickly towards the house and, after a few minutes, I climbed in at the same window. A servant girl carrying a lamp was leading the three men. They reached the door of Lord Brandir's room, broke it open and went in.

I followed them into the room. One of the men was pointing a gun at Lord Brandir, who was in his nightclothes. The other two were trying to open a large box.

'Tell me where the key is or I'll shoot you,' said the man with the gun. 'I'll count to ten, and then I'll shoot.'

'I won't tell you,' answered Lord Brandir fiercely. He was old but he did not look afraid.

The man began to count, 'One ... two ... three ...'

I ran quickly across the room and struck the man's gun with my stick. It fell to the ground. Then I brought the stick down on his head, and he fell on the floor.

The other two thieves came at me. One of them had a gun. Moving very fast, I picked up the man I had hit and held him in front of me. The thief fired at me, but the shot hit the other man, who died immediately. The other two thieves were small men. I seized them easily and tied their hands and feet.

The next morning, the two thieves were taken in front of a judge. They were well-known criminals and great enemies of the king. The judge was very pleased that I had caught them, and immediately wrote a letter to the king about it. Lord Brandir also told the king how I had caught the thieves.

That same afternoon a man came to take me to the king. I put on my best clothes and drank some beer, because my hands were shaking. Then I went to the palace, where the king was very kind to me, and told me I was a brave man. The queen, who was with him, looked at me with interest.

'So this is John Ridd,' she said. 'Dear Lorna has often spoken to me about you.'

'John Ridd,' said the king, 'you have done me a great service. Kneel!'

I went down on one knee, and he gently touched me on the shoulder.

'Stand, Sir John Ridd,' he said.

He had made me a knight.

Chapter 16   The Second Battle of the Valley

I was now allowed to go back to my farm a free man. I was sorry to leave Lorna, but glad to go back, because I was spending too much money in London. When I arrived home, the people of Oare organized a great dinner for me.

Winnie had brought Tom Faggus home safely, and he was now well again. Lizzie was going to marry one of Jeremy Stickles's officers.

Work continued as before. And, as before, the Doones came out of their valley and stole and killed. They went into the house of a man called Kit Badcock, killed his wife, carried away his baby and burned the house. This made the local people very angry. We had a meeting and decided that we must fight the Doones and end our troubles with them.

This was our plan. Somebody would tell the Doones that a man was going to carry a lot of gold along the road on a certain night. Of course, a group of Doones would go out to steal the gold. While they were away, a group of our men would attack the southern entrance to the valley. A second group would climb up the waterfall − the way I used to go when I saw Lorna. They would attack the valley from the other direction.

◆

The day arrived. That night, we heard that a group of Doones had left the valley to steal the gold. Then our men left for the southern entrance of the valley. A second group, including me, left for the waterfall. We managed to keep our guns out of the water as we climbed. We reached the top of the rock and went quickly over the fields. There was fighting at the southern entrance, but there were no Doone men in the valley.

We came to Carver's house and I saw a child there − Carver's son. I ran into the house and carried him out. Then we burned down the house. We called out all the women and children and then burned down the other houses.

'Doone town is burning!' cried the women. The whole valley was filled with red light.

As we had expected, the Doones ran back from the entrance, leaving only a few men there. We saw them clearly in the firelight, and my men shot at them as they came. I saw Kit Badcock kill Charlie Doone. It was Charlie who had carried off his child. I looked for Carver, but he was not among the Doones that night.

We did not hurt the Doone women or children, but many Doone men were killed that night. When morning came, only the Counsellor and Carver were alive. Every house in the valley was black and smoking.

◆

I must tell you the story of what happened to the rest of the Doones that same night.

Carver Doone led the group of Doones who went to steal the gold. We had sent a man to tell the Doones about the gold, and he went with them. He took them to an empty house. There they waited, and while they waited, our man poured water into their guns.

Suddenly a group of Oare men came to the door of the house. They pointed their guns at every Doone there. The Doones seized their own guns, but they could not fire them. The Doones fought bravely, but every one was killed except Carver, who jumped onto his great horse and rode away.

Chapter 17   The End of the Story

Soon after this, Lord Brandir died. The king gave his permission for Lorna to marry me. She came back from London, and everything was arranged for our marriage. Many people came to the wedding.

That day, Lorna looked more beautiful than I had ever seen

her. I put the wedding ring on her finger and she looked up at me. Just then, there was the sound of a shot and Lorna fell across my knees. There was blood on the white stone of the floor and on her white dress. Her face was white as snow, and she was cold, so cold. I placed her in my mother's arms and then I went out to find the man who had done this thing. I knew who it was – Carver!

I had no gun, only my hands to kill him with. I knew that Carver had a gun, but I did not care. Men moved quickly away from me as I rode up the hill. My horse flew like the wind and soon, in the distance, I saw a man on a great black horse. I knew that it was Carver.

'It's Carver's life or mine!' I said to myself.

I saw that he was carrying little Ensie, his son, in front of him. For some time he did not realize that I was following him. Then he came to a narrow passage in the rocks, turned and saw me. He tried to ride faster, but his horse was tired. He could not turn his horse round and fire, because the passage was too narrow. As I went past a tree, I pulled off a great branch and carried it with me.

Carver rode round a corner and came suddenly to the edge of the marsh. This part of the marsh is dangerous because there are areas of very soft, deep mud. Men have to go carefully there. If they don't, they can sink into the mud and disappear. Carver turned and fired his gun at me. The shot struck me somewhere, but I did not care. I thought of nothing but my enemy.

Suddenly, Carver rode straight at me. I struck his horse with the branch and the animal fell to the ground. Carver fell with it, and Lorna's diamond necklace fell from his pocket. For some minutes he could not get up. I jumped off my horse and seized the necklace. The little boy, Ensie, ran to me and looked up at me with fear in his eyes.

'Ensie, dear,' I said quietly, 'run back round the corner and find some flowers for the pretty lady in the church.'

He ran away. Carver stood up and looked round for his gun, but I had thrown it away. He only had his hands to fight with. I allowed him to come forward. Suddenly he seized me and broke a bone in my side. I caught his neck. He tried to free himself from my hands, but he could not move and I pushed him away.

'I'll stop now,' I said. 'You're beaten. Go – and learn to be a better man.'

But his feet had gone into the black mud. He went down very fast, deeper and deeper. The mud received him like the lips of death. He threw up his arms to heaven and there was terror on his face. I wanted to help him, but I was very weak after our fight and I could not save him.

He went down into the black mud and disappeared. It was the most terrible thing that I had ever seen.

◆

When the little boy came back with his flowers, there was only black mud where his father had been. I took him in my arms and climbed onto my horse.

I rode back home, feeling that I was in a dream. When I came to the door of my house, I fell off the horse. The women took the boy. Mother came out and helped me inside.

'He killed Lorna, and now I've killed him,' I said, giving her the necklace. 'Now let me see her. She's dead, but she's still mine.'

'She isn't dead,' said my mother. 'But you mustn't go to her like this, covered with blood.' She led me to my room.

For days, Lorna lay between life and death. I too was very ill because Carver had hurt me badly, but I only cared about Lorna. Why should I want to live without her? I looked at my hands, which had been so strong and now seemed as weak as a child's.

Slowly, Lorna came back to life. One morning the door opened, and my sister Annie came in. Behind her was Lorna.

Annie left, shutting the door behind her, and my wife came to me. She kissed me, and life returned to me.

And so the story ends. We sent Carver's son to school, and he is now a good, brave young man who thinks of me as his father. I will not say any more about the woman I love. But year after year, Lorna's beauty and kindness grow, and our love and happiness grow with it.

ACTIVITIES

Chapters 1–3

Before you read

1 Look at the pictures in the book. Which of these words do you think describe the book best? Give reasons for your opinion.

    a romantic

    b historical

    c detective

    d adventure

2 Find the words in *italics* in your dictionary. They are all in the story.

    a What is the connection between these and the law?

        hang   highwayman   outlaw

    b Which of these are connected with water? How?

        bush   drown   duck   marsh   mist   moor   waterfall   whirlpool

    c Look at these words:

        carriage   county   passage   weep   wrestle

        Which is the word for:

        – an area of land?

        – the act of crying?

        – the act of fighting?

        – a vehicle?

        – a place that joins two other places?

After you read

3 Are these sentences true or false? Correct the false ones.

    a John Ridd is twelve years old when he travels home across the moor.

    b There is a woman and a man in the carriage that John sees.

    c John's father was killed by John Fry.

    d John sees a Doone riding with a child across his horse.

    e Sir Ensor Doone lost his lands and became an outlaw.

    f The Doones are robbers and murderers who live in Oare.

    g When John is fifteen, he climbs up into the Doone valley.

    h Lorna tells John where he can hide from the Doones.

    i Tom Faggus and his horse, Winnie, save John's dog.

4 Discuss these questions.

    a What is the worst thing that happens to John in these chapters? What is the most exciting thing?

    b Is John right to want to kill Carver Doone?

Chapters 4–6

Before you read

5 Do you think John and Lorna will meet again? What kind of relationship will they have if they do? What kind of problems will they have?

6 Find these words in the dictionary. Use them in the sentences below.

    cannon   counsellor   guardian   hen   seize

    a The children are looked after by their ..... .

    b He ..... the money and ran out of the room.

    c They fired the ..... and killed four men.

    d The ..... did not give him very good advice.

    e Can you collect the eggs from the .....?

After you read

7 What do you know about these people?

    Lorna Doone   Lord Ensor Doone   The Counsellor

    Carver Doone   Uncle Reuben   Gwenny Carfax

8 Work in pairs. Act out the scene between Lorna Doone and Lord Alan Brandir.

Chapters 7–9

Before you read

9 How might Uncle Reuben be important in the future? Why might Lorna need John in the future? What do you think will happen between Carver and John?

10 Answer questions about the words in *italics*.

    a Is a *duke* a man or a woman?

    b Is a *rebel loyal* to the king?

    c Does a bird or a cow make a *nest*?

11 Answer these questions.

    a Why does Jeremy Stickles come to see John?

    b What questions does Judge Jeffreys ask John?

    c Why does Lorna need help?

    d What is John's connection with Tom Faggus?

    e What is the importance of the Duke of Monmouth in the story?

    f What makes Jeremy Stickles very frightened?

12 Discuss how Lorna's feelings for John change through these chapters. Whose feelings do you think are the strongest, Lorna's or John's?

Chapters 10–13

Before you read

13 What do you think will happen to the Doones? What do you think will happen to Lorna in the next part of the book?

14 Find these words in your dictionary. Which two are connected with fighting?

    battle   necklace   wound

After you read

15 Who says these words? What is the situation?

    a 'Will you promise never to see Lorna again?'

    b 'I didn't expect to see you again. I expected to die.'

    c 'If this was sold in London, you'd get a hundred thousand pounds.'

    d 'But I will kill you, unless you come back to the Doone valley tomorrow.'

    e 'Down! Down into the dust!'

    f 'Did you know that if you pass a glass necklace over milk, the milk will be creamier?'

    g 'If they ever find the owner, they'll return the lands to her.'

    h 'The men of Devon and Somerset are fighting each other.'

16 Discuss these questions.

    a Why do you think Carver wants to marry Lorna?

    b Were you surprised to hear Lorna's real story? Why/why not?

Chapters 14–17

Before you read

17 Do you think John will be able to marry Lorna? How can he do this when Lorna's family is so much better than his? What do you think will happen to Carver and the Doones?

18 Find the words in *italics* in your dictionary. Then correct the sentences.

    a When you *kneel*, you stand up.

    b A *knight* is a person with a low position in society.

After you read

19 Answer these questions.

    a Why does Lorna go to London?

    b What happens when John goes looking for Tom Faggus?

    c Why don't the soldiers hang John?

    d Why didn't John receive Lorna's letters?

    e Why does the king make John a knight?

    f What happens to Doone town?

    g What terrible thing does Carver do to Lorna?

    h What happens to Carver at the end of the story?

20 Do you think Carver and the Doone men deserve to die in the way they do? Give reasons for your opinion.

Writing

21 Which character in *Lorna Doone* do you like best? Who do you like least? Give reasons for your opinion.

22 Imagine that the story of *Lorna Doone* has just come out. Write about the new book for a newspaper. Give your opinion of it. Will other people enjoy it?

23 Imagine that you are Jeremy Stickles. Write about John Ridd. Then imagine that you are Gwenny Carfax. Write about John as you knew him.

24 Imagine that you are Lorna. You are living in London and John has not yet arrived. Write a letter to John. Tell him about your life in London and your feelings.

25 What part do these people or things play in the story? Choose two.
Annie   James II   the diamond necklace   Lord Wichehalse
Charlie Doone

26 Which parts of the book did you like best: the romantic parts, the historical parts or the action? Which scene did you find most exciting? Describe it and say why.